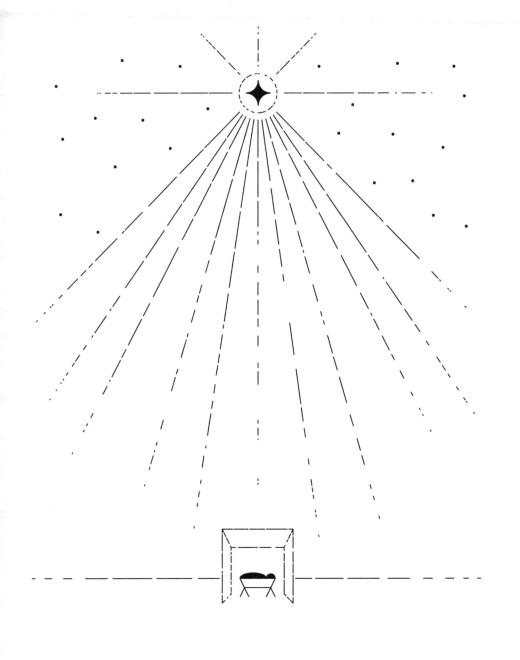

The GOD Who is WITH US

25-Day Devotional for

ADVENT

RONNIE MARTIN

Illustrated by NATHAN SCHROEDER

B&H
PUBLISHING
NASHVILLE, TENNESSEE

INTRODUCTION

This book is about nearness. And moments.

Particularly, it's about one moment in time when the nearness of God was made manifest to our weary world through the wondrous birth of His only begotten Son.

It's also about many other moments written to us in the pages of Scripture. Moments that remind us over and over again that God's fatherly desire has always been to draw near to us, His children, regardless of how rebellious we become and how resolute we are to create distance from Him.

Before we can blink, January will arrive, and Christmastime will have faded into memory as the New Year beckons us back to our detached and divided lives. My hope is that this book will help you spend some time reflecting on all the moments God has been near to you over the past year. Maybe it was difficult to trace His heart during some of the more turbulent times you experienced. Maybe you had moments where God seemed aloof and His presence felt obscured because of some heartbreaking occurrences that painted the year with an unwanted depth of sadness and sobriety.

Whatever the moment, God has given us the gift of hindsight to see that, through it all, He was with us in it all. As the hope and promise of Christmas begins its yearly sparkle, would you look back with me for a moment so we can look forward in hope to all the unknown moments that are already known by our loving and gracious Lord? Moments that we attempt to recapture every December as the hustle and bustle of Christmastime threaten to dim the bright promise the holiday is intended to reflect, which is that we have been visited by the God who is with us.

Merry Christmas to you and yours,

Ronnie Martin

BEFORE THE FOUNDATION

In the beginning, God . . .

GENESIS 1:1

B efore you read another word.

Look up from the page, and spend some time reflecting on these origin words from the book of Genesis: *In the beginning, God.* Most of the time, you would have already wandered ahead without contemplating why God chose to begin all of Scripture with these particular, and maybe even peculiar, words.

What thoughts spring to mind as you consider the words *In the beginning, God*? Maybe images of a darkened, murky, uncreated world without landscapes, architecture, animals, or humans. Maybe the word *beginning* recalls the opening scenes of a memorable film or the first pages of a favorite novel. Perhaps it is difficult for you to imagine what a *beginning* even looked like before God spoke our world into being? What is most important for us is not necessarily what it was like before God began forming the world, but that God was already there. Before He supernaturally declared the world into existence from an unimaginable nothingness, God *was*.

As we allow ourselves a few moments to imagine the beginning of our world, perhaps the most significant detail to note is that Scripture doesn't allow us to imagine it without the presence of God. Before anything, there was something: God. Even more astonishingly, before *the beginning* ever was, God had already chosen you to be a necessary part of it.

> He chose us in him before the foundation of the world. (Eph. 1:4a).

As a songwriter, I get ideas for lyrics and melodies in abstract and unique ways that seem to defy any sort of objective formula or rational explanation. As much as I wish inspiration would come prepackaged in a monthly subscription, it insists on being more ghostlike in nature. Before a lyric or melody is conceived or composed in my consciousness, an image will materialize from any variety of sources to comprise the grain of a song that will someday become realized in recorded fruition.

Very incompletely, this illustrates our *chosen-ness* by God. Before He had ever composed the opening notes that would comprise His creation song, He had imagined you in His unfathomably infinite mind to "be fruitful and multiply and fill the earth and subdue it, and have dominion over the fish of the sea and over the birds of the heavens and over every living thing that moves on the earth" (Gen. 1:28). Equally as thought-provoking is this stunning realization: not only did God choose you before He chose the world He would create, but He also planned what our purpose would be as His chosen people.

> . . . that we should be holy and blameless before him. (Eph. 1:4b)

To be a chosen son or daughter of God is to become holy and blameless, or to say it another way, set apart *before Him* and *for Him*. The reason God chose you to be holy and blameless is because He can only make His home with those who are set apart and righteous like Himself.

Of course, God knew that when He chose you, another decision had to be made to ensure that His presence with you would remain.

> In love he predestined us for adoption to himself as sons through Jesus Christ, according to the purpose of his will. (Eph. 1:5)

So there it is. That troublesome word, in all of its winsome and wintry glory: *predestine*.

It makes some of us either mildly or wildly uncomfortable, but what the apostle Paul intended when he wrote to the church in Ephesus was not to begin a theological debate but to assure them that *belonging to God* didn't happen by some random stroke of luck. No, God loved us before He made us and planned to adopt us because the sinful status we were born into meant God wasn't automatically our Father at birth. So to be *predestined* means that *in the beginning God* meant for you to be His, and for Him to be with you because He imagined you, loved you, chose you, planned for you, and purposed to be with you.

Forever.

So as you look with either happy anticipation or nervous dread toward Christmas and New Year's, remember that none of your beginnings will begin in the absence of God's presence. In the same way that God was present before He created the world, God will continue to go before you in all things. This helps remind you that all those beginning things that cause so much fear, unrest, and anxiety will not be entered into alone or carried out in isolation.

Before your beginning, God had already begun planning your creation and salvation. And He has plans for this new beginning as well.

PAUSE, PONDER, AND PRAY

CLOTHED BY GOD

And the LORD God made for Adam and for his wife
garments of skins and clothed them.

GENESIS 3:21

Ponder for a moment what it must have been like to be *clothed by God*. Hours earlier, heartbreaking words had been introduced into the dictionary of the world—*fear, guilt,* and *shame*. Lying in ruins were two grief-stricken souls from our original family of origin. A sorrowful man and woman who could now only possess memories of the ageless energy, undimmed joy, and childlike contentment that would remain unachieved by innumerable generations of sons and daughters from that day forth.

For those of us familiar with the tragic chapter of Adam and Eve, it's hard to read this end portion of the story and not feel the nakedness and regret that was surely emanating from their heartsick souls. Sin had entered the door of the world, and Adam and Eve were responsible for creating it. We can all reflect on a story in our lives that we wish we could reverse—an unwise decision that changed the course of our existence forever or an unkind word that harmed a dear relationship that has never been repaired. Adam and Eve had experienced a utopian earth that they and their offspring would no longer get to enjoy. Contemplating the enormity of this loss must have been overwhelming.

Still, will you wonder with me for a minute? Because maybe there is a more hopeful way for us to read and receive this verse? A more redemptive perspective would be to notice how God did not abandon Adam and Eve in their cataclysmic loss of innocence but showed His most fatherly love for them by clothing them in their newfound nakedness.

I remember when I was a toddler and my mother would give me and my little brother a bath during the winter months of Southern California when it would dip down to frigid sixty-degree temperatures. We would step out of the bath dripping wet and teeth chattering, and she would wrap a towel around each of us before we ran like banshees down the stairs to the fireplace, where we would sit in our miniature rocking chairs as the warmth of the embers thawed our shivering limbs. Like Adam and Eve, we weren't left in the coldness of our nakedness. We had been covered. Clothed.

As you find yourself at the end of another year that may have exposed your own nakedness, how might you like to be "clothed"? Maybe you already bear the weight of another twelve months that you feel were squandered by bad luck and unfortunate circumstances. Perhaps you look back and see so many missed opportunities and a New Year that would be so much different had you just made some wiser decisions. Or maybe you feel disappointed because you had hoped for something new on the horizon that never materialized. It could be that you experienced some profound loss, and you are entering January with the stark realization that loneliness and limitations are once again your unwanted companions.

What you'll find from our heavenly Father is One who wants to clothe you. He wants to cover the fear, guilt, and shame that characterized the past year and threatens to repeat the pattern as the New Year beckons. In either the quiet or the cacophony of this present moment, we remember that the same God who clothed and covered Adam and Eve in their guilt and shame will not leave you unclothed in yours.

> As you wait for the revealing of our Lord Jesus Christ, who will sustain you to the end, guiltless in the day of our Lord Jesus Christ. God is faithful, by whom you were called into the fellowship of his Son, Jesus Christ our Lord. (1 Cor. 1:7–9)

You are covered.

PAUSE, PONDER, AND PRAY

WHEREVER YOU GO

Behold, I am with you and will keep you wherever you go,
and will bring you back to this land. For I will not leave you
until I have done what I have promised you.

GENESIS 28:15

Jacob the Wrestler is the story of another man who confirms to us that the lives of our biblical heroes were nothing short of blotchy, muddled messes. Over and over again, we are reminded of how surprisingly human they were. Of how uncomfortably comfortable we cozy up alongside them.

By the way, if you're anything like me, you find it oddly comforting that these are the kind of suspiciously odd specimens God used to reveal His plans and keep His promises.

Who is this God who not only calls crazy people to carry out His will but stays with them when it looks like they're doing everything in their will to try and thwart it? Who is this God? This is the God of Christmas past, present, and future. The God who is with you, who keeps you, and who brings you back, full stop. God will not leave you with any of His promises unkept, even when it seems like they're hanging precariously in suspenseful unfulfillment.

Jacob was a man chock-full of life's rational and irrational fears. Fear of the future, fear for the safety of his family, fear of an unresolved relationship with his more ruggedly aggressive twin brother Esau, who gave Jacob some good reasons to tremble a bit. Okay, maybe Jacob had some rational fears after all. But the reason for Jacob's fears, and for our own, is that the future cannot be grasped, controlled, maintained, or called to do what we command of it. Because of this, we worry about what we cannot see. We try to control that which is impossible to grasp firmly. We are so much like Jacob, wrestling with God over things we try to maneuver or manipulate but in actuality cannot because of our flesh-and-blood inability to perform the supernatural, as much as this tendency bleeds from our natural self.

So we, like Jacob, need someone to be with us, to keep us, to bring us back, and to never leave us with unkept promises. We need a God who will never forsake us,

So we can confidently say,

"The Lord is my helper;
I will not fear;
what can man do to me?" (Heb. 13:6)

I wonder what thoughts might be traveling through your mind today as the past year fades into memory, and the new year looms on the horizon with all of its hoped-for peaks and potentially harrowing valleys? If you're like Jacob, you might be tempted to spend this season wandering through a series of unsettled wonderings, unable to grasp the presence of God that has been all-pervasive but not always perceived.

Behold, I am with you and will keep you.

Maybe those words feel like distant echoes in the chambers of your mind and it turns out that you have way more in common with this Old

Testament wrestler than you care to admit. You desperately want to hear God bless you while you make another futile attempt to gain control of a life that you will never master on your own. Christmastime has a way of reminding us of these less-than-Christmassy realities.

Because, in the burst of a moment, the world will come to a halt, and you will be left with a limp like Jacob. Your encounter with God on the wrestling mat has altered you physically, but it has also changed you internally and spiritually. These sleepless hours of transcendent toil have given you a glimpse of your Creator's fathomless care. You have found someone who exposes your vainglorious scheming and fruitless manipulations, but will never lose you as you lose your way. You will be kept, like a treasured possession, secured and preserved from all the wicked devices that threaten to lure you away on both the inside and the outside.

Behold the One who will undo you in order to do this characteristic work of His heart and hands within you. Behold the One who calms your fears, upholds your arms, and stays by your side as unfailingly as the morning light appears as a welcoming friend at the dawn of every new day.

For I will not leave you.

Enter this uncharted New Year with newfound courage. You have never been less alone.

PAUSE, PONDER, AND PRAY

ADVENT DAY 4

FOR GOOD

As for you, you meant evil against me, but God meant it
for good, to bring it about that many people should be kept
alive, as they are today. So do not fear; I will provide for
you and your little ones.
GENESIS 50:20–21

A s you begin reading today, reflect on a time when you felt most undeserving of God's kindness. Maybe a horrible situation arose as the result of a disastrous decision you made, and your mind sank into a condemnation-filled mire of thoughts that culminated in this: *I'm going to get what I deserve now.* What comes to mind in these moments is that we will surely get our just desserts. What often doesn't come to mind is that we may just get what we don't deserve.

How quickly we forget that Jesus Christ and the Calvary cross are the only reasons we don't get what we deserve! Of course, our forgetfulness is due to the reputation our heart has gained for being a devil of deceit. It convinces us to believe that our sins are like bargaining tools with God. A grandiose sin calls for a grandiose punishment. A miniature infraction will bring barely a glance from God. How we maximize our transgressions! How we minimize them!

Genesis 50 contains the dilemma of Joseph's brothers who were still replete with regret. Years after grace and forgiveness were granted them, doubt still seeped through all of the unhealed crevices. Joseph speaks words of loveliness that echo the grace of the Lord: "God meant it for good."

Let those words stay suspended in midair for a moment or two. God *meant* it. God *means* for the bad things we do to become the good things He has done. That *doneness* is meant to create an indescribable flurry of weightless joy inside us. That *doneness* lifts the guilt-ridden, yearning-for-grace anvil you carry on your shoulders so that you might look back and say FOR GOOD! in all caps. That *doneness* redeems all the doings you did that created the disrepair you never wanted. That *doneness* reminds you that there is no fear of abandonment from God because His name is synonymous with the word *Provider*.

Let's be clear about something else, though. Here's what God's *doneness* doesn't do. It doesn't ignore the trials and trauma that have blown through your life like a bitterly unwelcome winter wind. It does mean that although *we don't know why* God allows our lives to be subject to harm, we know that it is not because He is uncaring or unwise, since He sent Christ to endure unimaginable suffering for the sake of glory and salvation. Although we don't know *why*, we know *who*, and knowing *who* is infinitely more valuable when we consider that the One we know is working all things "together for good, for those who are called according to his purpose" (Rom. 8:28). That's not a Band-Aid for a broken limb, either. That's a promise for all of us brokenhearted, wounded, and damaged people who have become the people of a compassionate God who has never made an arbitrary decision in His existence.

So today, on the eve of another merry-ish Christmas and happy-ish New Year, with all of our rational and irrational fears dotting our hearts like the Milky Way, we remember that we don't need to fear, even if our fears currently cloak us like thick-knitted winter blankets. The same grace Joseph had on his brothers who meant him evil is the grace God has for us who were born:

> You were dead in the trespasses and sins in which you once walked. . . . But God, being rich in mercy, because of the great love with which he loved us, even when we were dead in our trespasses, made us alive together with Christ—by grace you have been saved— and raised us up with him and seated us with him in the heavenly places in Christ Jesus, so that in the coming ages he might show the immeasurable riches of his grace in kindness toward us in Christ Jesus. (Eph. 2:1–7)

Whatever rational or irrational fears are hovering over your heart this season, remember the One who holds them firmly in His grasp. And means them for your good and His glory.

PAUSE, PONDER, AND PRAY

BECOMING COURAGEOUS

Have I not commanded you? Be strong and courageous.
Do not be frightened, and do not be dismayed, for the LORD
your God is with you wherever you go.
JOSHUA 1:9

We know what it's like to be afraid when we are standing at the foot of a mountain we feel we have no business climbing. We have all been tasked with something that reaches far beyond our level of comfort, where we feel like we are operating outside of our gift mix, until someone steps in who believes in us and encourages us to try. This was the story of Joshua after God called him to replace Moses as the leader of God's people.

Granted, the text doesn't say Joshua experienced the kind of debilitating doubt many of us experience when we are called to do frighteningly courageous things. But God charged Joshua nonetheless and encouraged him to be strong and courageous, which is an odd color scheme when matched with our monotone-like dismay.

Of course, the reason God said it was possible for Joshua to succeed in taking on the monumental task of leading the Israelites is because God had no expectation that Joshua would undertake this task alone. No, the Lord would be with him. *Wherever you go.*

Put your mind on pause for a brief moment and think about the profundity of that statement. "Wherever you go," God told Joshua, "The LORD your God is with you." Sometimes in the frantic nature, fearful symmetry, and sunken depths of our proneness to wander, we forget there is no place we go in our lives where God has not gone ahead of us in glorious procession. "Wherever you go," God whispers to us when that foot takes another step into unknown forests of tangled branches that obscure our sight and cloud our direction. "Wherever you go," God whispers when the darkness descends upon us in the night hours, and we know that dawn won't provide the light we long for.

> "Wherever you go," God whispers. "The LORD *your* God is with you."

Let honesty be your friend, and admit that you have fashioned some gods this year. You have built altars and bowed down to a vibrant assortment of objects, people, desires, and ambitions. Truthfully, they've not resembled God all that much, but they have received your worship, your love, your adoration, and your allegiance. The problem with these lower-case "g" gods is that none of them are the capital-G God of the universe, as much as you've tried to make them the god of *your* universe. In fact, they're not really gods at all, no matter how much you've exalted them to the stained-glass spires of your heart and mind. Ponder now the Lord of the universe, the capital-G God who is *with you wherever you go*. With you through all the great unknowns that await in the New Year, while remembering that unknowns are only *unknown* to you. How much greater to have His presence than all those cheap imitations!

So when the Lord your God encourages you to be strong and courageous, you can embrace those two inconceivable postures. You can see them as not moments for you to pass or fail because it's not really you, but "he who is in you," who "is greater than he who is in the world" (1 John 4:4) will transform you into the person you have no possibility of becoming on your own. Regardless of the outcome, you can trust the Lord who controls the times and seasons of all things, including the outcomes. So . . .

Breathe out your angst.

Breathe in His approval.

Because the God who goes before you upholds you in times of faithfulness and faithlessness, belief and doubt, joy and despair, courage and fear. *Wherever you go.*

He is closer to you than the skin on your bones.

PAUSE, PONDER, AND PRAY

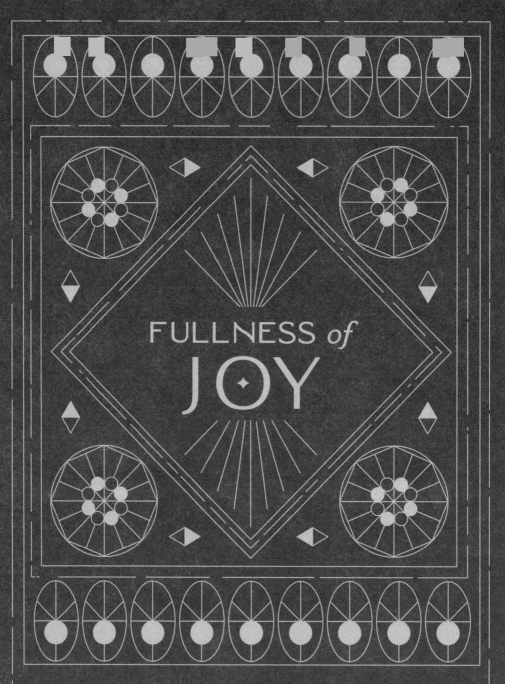

FULLNESS *of*
JOY

Psalm 16:11

IN HIS PRESENCE

*You make known to me the path of life; in your presence
there is fullness of joy; at your right hand are pleasures
forevermore.*
PSALM 16:11

When you reflect on the past year, who or what would you say had the greatest influence on you? Maybe it was a colleague at work, a fellow student at your school or university, or a spouse, family member, or friend? Maybe it was less relational. It could be that you spent a lot of time on social media or tucked away into a corner reading books or journaling your thoughts? Perhaps you surrounded yourself with something more shameful and unmentionable, and it has continued to have an influential role on your spiritual, emotional, and physical well-being.

David the psalmist was longing for the everlasting things we forever long for but end up searching for in people, places, and particulars that are not able to fill the ocean-like depths of our longing. In the same way a solitary drop of water is unable to quench an insatiable, desert-like thirst, the shallow feeding troughs of vacuous pleasures will never meet our desires. David's bottomless desires match our bottomless desires. He wants to be preserved through life's storms; he wants to know he has a beautiful inheritance; he wants counsel and instruction; and he wants the Lord to lead him through every step he takes through the lowest valleys and loftiest visions. Like us, David wants to know that everything is going to be all right because God is with him through all the not all right things the world will level squarely at us.

David knows that in himself he will not always know the right path to take that will lead to the satisfaction of his innermost longings. So he looks to the only person he knows can provide the most lasting satisfaction to his everlasting yearnings.

You make known to me.

Whether he feels it or not, David understands that life-filled paths, joy-filled presence, and forever-fulfilling pleasures can only be discovered at the source. Just like the history of a beautiful piece of fruit can be traced to a healthy vine rooted in well-watered soil, only the Creator of such wonders can be trusted to provide them for those who come seeking them. David the psalmist reminds us that *longing* is a God-given gift for His children who seek their desires from the Giver of satisfaction.

Think about a time when a long day of labor culminated in the reward of a great meal and a much-needed night of fellowship with good friends. If you are like me and you love good (and, okay, even "bad") food, the anticipation of what I am going to eat is almost as good as eating itself. Not only that, but if I knew the meal was going to be eaten in isolation, the food wouldn't taste half as good as it would if I knew I'd be sharing it with loved ones. In Jesus Christ, we receive a bounty of these undeserved delicacies! Not only do we get to look forward to the meal but also to the person who will share the meal, who also happens to be the One who provided everything that's indescribably inviting and nourishing on the table.

But a sobering thought to give some additional time to is this: there can be no fullness of joy at the table unless Christ is sitting at the head of it.

Do you long for things to be different as the New Year looms on the horizon? Do you wish you could stop trying to satisfy your longing with people, places, and particulars that have no power to placate them? David the psalmist shows us the possibilities that await when we reorder the eyes of our hearts to ones that are

> looking to Jesus, the founder and perfecter of our faith, who for the joy that was set before him endured the cross, despising the shame, and is seated at the right hand of the throne of God. (Heb. 12:2)

In the same way that during the spring and summer months we flee from the drab shadows to reposition ourselves under the pleasant rays of the sun, we reset our wandering gaze upon Jesus over and over again. Like David, we declare, "With you is the fountain of life; in your light do we see light" (Ps. 36:9), because we know that "the children of mankind take refuge in the shadow of your wings. They feast on the abundance of your house, and you give them drink from the river of your delights" (Ps. 36:7b–8).

Embrace this undiminished joy that is found in the ever-enduring Perfecter of our faith.

PAUSE, PONDER, AND PRAY

NEVER LEAVE OR FORSAKE

*Keep your life free from love of money, and be content with
what you have, for he has said, "I will never leave you nor
forsake you."*
HEBREWS 13:5

M oney. We should almost refer to it as the "M word," shouldn't
we?

Take a moment to reflect on the kind of relationship you have
cultivated with this dangerously fickle companion over the past year,
regardless of whether it was the occasion for feast or famine. How
would you say the abundance or lack of money influenced the curves
and contours of your heart? How did it alter your present dilemmas
and future aspirations? Did it surface a more fragile sense of security
than you ever imagined? Perhaps you are on the brink of financial ruin,
and a scarcity of funds is proving to be the greatest threat to your live-
lihood you've ever known. Or perhaps last year was one for the record
books, and you got a new job or promotion that's totally changed your
ability to acquire things you want.

Here is what we must remember when emotional entanglements
with money send tingles of joy or shudders of fear up our spines: God
has an intricate and compassionate understanding of what we need

in this world in order to endure. We know that money is not an evil entity in and of itself, but Scripture is clear that the *love* of money—whether from abundance or lack—should be guarded against, as it is "a root of all kinds of evils. It is through this craving that some have wandered away from the faith and pierced themselves with many pangs" (1 Tim. 6:10).

The reason we are so easily seduced by an unhealthy, idolatrous love of monetary wealth is because we believe it provides insurance against poverty, as well as an enchanted entrance into the realization of all we have ever dreamed of. Of course, money does indeed offer some fragment of natural security against poverty. It is also true that money can be a sanctified instrument ordained by the heart of God that allows us to attain some of the material or experiential things we have always imagined attaining. God is a good Father who has a thing for good gifts, after all.

But what money will never possess is the divine ability to provide contentment of the soul. Money makes "a strange bedfellow" as some might say. Although it can purchase a comfortable bed, it can never compensate for a discomfort that envelops the soul. The writer of the book of Hebrews seeks to illuminate our hearts so we see that money is a lousy companion as we amble through the more critical moments of life. Rather, we need a spiritually transcendent presence that can be counted on so that contentedness becomes the characteristic of our soul, regardless of how heavy our bankroll is.

Does the accumulation of money have your soul cowering in the clutches of its subtle death grip? It may not be that your heart has a love affair with money as much as your hands need it to simply survive. Maybe you have come to the realization that the acquisition of more money and more opportunity has dominated the spiritual tranquility of your thought life and strained all the Christ-exalting affections out of your heart. Whatever state of fiscal peril you find yourself in as the calendar page turns the corner into January, remember these words from Jesus:

I will never leave you nor forsake you. (Heb. 13:5)

What money could never provide has been provided by the promise of an everlasting presence that brings the kind of peace money can only falsely promise. Someday we may all shudder in horror when we consider the shameful value we placed in something as illusory and unreliable as money. How we looked to its fragility to be our stability. How we put our hope in it to satisfy the fathomless well of hunger and thirst that characterizes the depths of our spiritual passions.

I will never leave you nor forsake you.

Say those words. Pray those words. Believe those words. Because they come from the wellspring of a heart that wants you to be fulfilled by the Filler of fullness.

PAUSE, PONDER, AND PRAY

YOU CAN DO NOTHING

"I am the vine; you are the branches. Whoever abides in me
and I in him, he it is that bears much fruit, for apart from
me you can do nothing."
JOHN 15:5

We absolutely abhor the thought of ourselves being as astonishingly needy as we are, don't we? The stark but saving revelation of the Christian life is that, in and of ourselves, we don't possess "the stuff" we need to survive and thrive in our sin-soaked world. We are fragile, feeble, and unfaithful creatures who only took a breath this morning because God graciously decided to provide another moment's worth of oxygen for our aging lungs.

It is hard for us to imagine that we are really this incapable, this unable, this utterly weak and disturbingly dependent. Perhaps you have had a "capable" year. You hit some of your unachievable markers, achieved some of your impossible to reach goals, and even got around to checking off a bucket list item or two. If this describes you, put this beautifully illustrated Advent book down immediately and rejoice to the God of your good fortune! This is certainly not a year to look back on and be ashamed of, but it may be one that requires you to ask yourself just how much self-assurance these achievements have instilled in you as you face the dawning of a new year that may have fewer appealing arrangements in store for you.

Here is what we know about the unimaginable graciousness of Jesus Christ. He doesn't want us to have an opinion of ourselves that is ultimately going to harm our deception-riddled hearts. Our fiercely fought-for autonomy and rough-hewn individualism do not possess the weight we need to anchor us when the storms of our existence rail against the sails of our self-reliance. Life will eventually turn into tragic novels and illustrate to us that the independence our world (American society, in particular) has held up as the ideal is merely the stuff of myths and legends.

But Jesus tells us something about Himself that is of utmost good for ourselves. We are branches. And not only branches but brittle branches who need a lifelong attachment to a life-sustaining vine. We are not self-sustaining, self-propelling, perpetual-motion machines. On a physical and somewhat hilarious level, none of us can even survive for that many hours without food, water, and shelter of some kind. From rich to poor, famous to anonymous, we all need these essentials to withstand the internal and external elements of our essence. On a spiritual level, we are no less needy. We need the life vine of Jesus Christ to produce the fruit-bearing branches we were always meant to become since Eden. Apart from Christ, we can produce something that will resemble edible fruit but will be found to be disgustingly rotten on the inside. Hear the words of Jesus whispering softly but assuredly to you right now,

Apart from me you can do nothing.

If it was anybody else, you might react with something to the effect of, "Hey, you must think pretty highly of yourself if you think I should be *that* dependent on you!" And yet, because this is Jesus, we know His words are meant to tell us something important about our

reality so that His reality becomes more real to us. Would you consider the simple words of that last sentence again? The reality of Jesus
is more real than the sensation you feel on the tips of your fingers
when you touch another human being.

Think of how different the New Year might be if your single greatest pursuit was to abide in the presence of Jesus more fully and wonderfully? To endure, remain, and persevere with the Shepherd of your
soul. Think of what the fruit of your life might taste like when you
come to the end of the following year. Imagine how the people around
you might be affected if you were so affected by this gracious and
merciful truth.

You can do nothing.

But think of the something you will become as you remain
rooted to the vine where His love, grace, mercy, and compassion will
strengthen and nourish your spiritual limbs. Think of the something
you are becoming when you embrace the everything He is and ever
will be for you and in you for all eternity.

That you can do nothing without Him is everything.

PAUSE, PONDER, AND PRAY

IN TIME OF NEED

Let us then with confidence draw near to the throne of
grace, that we may receive mercy and find grace to help in
time of need.
HEBREWS 4:16

One night when I was eight years old, I laid my troubled head down on my feathery pillow. As hard as I tried, I couldn't fall asleep because an unfinished homework assignment was plaguing my tender conscience. Eventually, I began to cry, and somehow, my father heard the sound of my boyhood tears.

In no time, he came into the room I shared with my younger brother, and with his loving but low rumbling voice, asked what was troubling me. In my adolescent distress, I confessed to him all that I was feeling in that sleepless hour. What happened next was unexpected. He promptly pulled me out of bed, brought me into the living room, and pulled me in close under his arm as we snuggled up on the couch. Initially, I was afraid since I could only imagine he was going to reprimand me about my unfinished assignment. I soon realized all my fears were unfounded. He didn't lash out at me; he laughed.

Not in a way that was dismissive of my dilemma but to communicate to me that I had his mercy and grace in my time of need. "Don't worry, sometimes things like this happen," is what he said. "Tell you what, why don't I wake you up a little earlier than usual in the morning, and you can try to finish your paper before you leave for school?" This was not at all what I was expecting. My expectation was a mad dad chastising me for not finishing my school assignment because I had procrastinated by playing with my friends and riding my BMX bike, which, truth be told, were far more enjoyable activities. Instead, he looked right through me and laughed. It was a profound laugh filled with the profundity of unmerited mercy. It was so characteristic of my other Father. It was a laugh that gave me confidence that I could finish my assignment because I wasn't worried that a punishment was imminent. I could draw near because He drew near to me. I wasn't a fourth-grade student trembling in fear on the couch that night; I was the beloved son of John Francis Martin.

Brothers and sisters, this is an imperfect picture of the grace and mercy of King Jesus, who sits on the most approachable of thrones to give us what we can in confidence know we will receive. Not because we deserve to receive it but because He who is most deserving releases it to the most undeserving. That's us, by the way.

If you are a human being—and you are—the past year has been filled with moments that you desperately wish you could recover. Whether it was a callous remark that caused relational harm, a careless mistake at work that damaged your reputation severely, an impulsive monetary move that cost you financially, or a year in which you all but ignored your relationship with God in favor of other, less godlike interests. Whatever it was, the writer of Hebrews tells us something more important about God than what we know about ourselves, which is that He sits on a throne of shockingly forgiving grace. This means that instead of being like an angry Greek god who is glaring at you, waiting to punish you for another round of royal screwups, He beckons you to come close in your time of need because the only thing He has for you is another offering of love, mercy, and grace.

In time of need.

The benefit of spiritual maturity is that it provides this revelation to us: we exist perpetually in a time of need. Sure, the severity of our need may fluctuate depending on a host of alternating circumstances throughout the currents of life, but there is never a moment when the sun dawns or the moon rises that we are not in need of God and all His good provision. Sadly, we like to believe there are some days when God can go ahead and take the day off. We feel confident that our efforts are more than adequate for the tasks ahead, but it's a faithless, wisdom-less confidence. It's a confidence that refuses to take into consideration the fact that we possess no powers of telepathy to know what the next hour will deliver to our doors. The confidence the writer of Hebrews mentions is one that exists in a heart that knows what it has no ability to produce, which is divinely ordained help from the One who holds our time in His hands (Ps. 31:15) and who "knows our frame; he remembers that we are dust" (Ps. 103:14). Our times and our frames are held together by "the Word [who] became flesh" (John 1:14), who "spoke, and it came to be" (Ps. 33:9) and "intricately [wove us] in the depths of the earth" (Ps. 139:15).

I'm no great theologian, but nothing in that language suggests we are anything but needy creatures who have a deeply unneedy and merciful Creator, a Creator who welcomes us to come to Him with a confidence that is even provided by Him. What might it change for you as you contemplate the depths of this profound invitation by Jesus?

Imagine for a moment that you could bring to King Jesus whatever has caused you to shudder this past year. And as you bring it to Him, He runs to you, pulls you in close, and tells you everything is going to be okay. Whatever you did or did not accomplish is not so all-encompassing that it falls outside His infinite capacity for love, mercy, and grace that washes over you like an everlasting fountain.

Imagine that.

Or better yet, believe it. And then run with abandon to the most approachable throne in your most critical time of need.

Which is every day.

PAUSE, PONDER, AND PRAY

AWAY FROM GOD

But Jonah rose to flee to Tarshish from the presence of the
LORD. He went down to Joppa and found a ship going to
Tarshish. So he paid the fare and went down into it, to go
with them to Tarshish, away from the presence of the LORD.
JONAH 1:3

I have the good pleasure of sharing with you one of the most ridiculous
stories ever from my childhood. I was passing by my friend Dawn's
house one morning when I saw her walk through the front door and
throw a piece of her mother's fine china down onto the driveway
where it shattered into a thousand pieces. She asked me if I wanted to
join her, and since breaking dishes still seems fun even today, I followed
her into the dining room where we proceeded to clean out all of her
family's dishes, bowls, cups, and saucers.

We were about five minutes into our violence against kitchen-
ware campaign when I heard a thundering voice in the form of Dawn's
mother shouting from the top of the stairs, "DAWN, WHAT HAVE
YOU DONE??!!"

Being the not-very-intelligent boy that I was, I took that as my
cue to mosey on down the street and see how things were going at
the Martin household. I entered my house with stealth-like elegance,

made a brilliantly muted beeline for my dad's office, and promptly hid myself under his work desk. Of course, it didn't take long for my dad to hunt me down, discover my crafty hideaway, and inform me that breaking another family's priceless dinnerware was not exactly the smartest decision I could have made that day.

Two ironies. The first was that I *knew* I had done something wrong. My heart was thumping like a bass drum in my tiny, six-year-old chest. The second is that when I got home I immediately hid under the one place my dad spent a rather large amount of time—his office desk! But in my rationally irrational kid mind, this was going to be my safe haven. Of course, I can laugh at the absurdity of it all now, but it's no less absurd than what Jonah did when he boarded an ocean liner going in the opposite direction that God had commanded him to go.

Jonah had a fearful task ahead. God had told him to preach repentance against a nation he would have preferred to be judged unmercifully instead. Ironically, Jonah was a prophet who was well acquainted with the grace and mercy of God and assumed that if the Ninevites repented after hearing his incredibly short sermon—"Yet forty days, and Nineveh shall be overthrown!" (Jonah 3:4)—God would gladly and mercifully spare them. The problem was that Jonah didn't want this enemy nation of the Israelites spared! So he tried to flee from the presence of God, which in some ways is the equivalent of trying to flee from the presence of air but even less possible.

I wonder if this could describe you in some way, shape, or form? It may be possible that anger or shame has you running in some wildly remote directions to the degree that you feel like you are successfully escaping the inescapable phenomenon of God's omnipresence. The unique thing about God's people, and one of the things that makes them uniquely God's people, is that they don't have the power to pull themselves away from the presence of God. Even in the throes of our darkest and deadliest sins, God is there. Even in the disheartening aftermath of every questionable decision, God is there. Everywhere we go is everywhere God is.

In our shame we attempt to flee from His presence, but even when we feel the dimmest light of it illuminating our darkly concealed edges, it is still there in glimmering sharpness, waiting to expose our shallow desires to escape, while embracing our stubborn refusal to enter back in. God is inescapable. Praise God! The worst thing in the world would be for us to exist in the absence of God's presence. So horrible is that reality that this is the final reality for all those who die in unrepentant sin.

Are you in a fleeing place right now? Do you feel like you have gotten *away from God*? Although it may feel like the opposite for a moment, a *fleeing* place is not a freeing place. Jonah did not experience the freedom he desired when he boarded that ship to Tarshish; rather, he became enslaved, which is always the result when we obey our whims and desires.

Paul wrote a letter to the church in Galatia to remind them that "for freedom Christ has set us free; stand firm therefore, and do not submit again to a yoke of slavery" (Gal. 5:1). When you think of the New Year fast approaching, what kind of whims and desires do you feel enslaved to? Does your life resemble millions of glass shards lying scattered across the last or lost year of your life because you've never stopped running and never started listening to the voice of the Lord who desires to reroute you to the place He has called you?

Let God's presence not push you away but pull you back into communion with Him, because the mercy He had for His stubborn prophet Jonah is the mercy you have waiting for you if you would just stop running in the wrong direction.

There is no *away from* when you have a God who refuses to stay away from you.

PAUSE, PONDER, AND PRAY

CREATE IN ME

Create in me a clean heart, O God, and renew a right spirit
within me. Cast me not away from your presence, and take
not your Holy Spirit from me. Restore to me the joy of your
salvation, and uphold me with a willing spirit.
PSALM 51:10–12

Have you ever spiraled to the end of some downward descent in your life until you finally made one blunder too many, and the final misstep was an irrevocably costly one? David has come to a place in his life where he can't step forward until he stops looking back. Meaning, he desperately needs the intervention of divine forgiveness so his pleas to God for renewal and restoration will be heeded and granted. It is the right prayer at the right time because it's never the wrong time to pray to God to renew and restore what we have utterly and completely fractured.

At times our transgressions can be so severe that they send a spiritual shock wave through the undisclosed chambers of our mind. We almost can't believe we did what we did, said what we said, or thought what we thought. These moments of self-revelation are how the Holy Spirit begins to soften the bristly perimeters of our briary hearts that have been buried knee-deep in unconfessed sin.

David finds himself in a predicament like this where he needs to face God in all of the shame of his dreadful disgrace. What would the wages be for these horrifying atrocities? How could he ever go back to being a man after God's own heart? We wonder the same thing when we have sinned so sharply before God that it feels beyond all hope and imagination that He could ever draw near to us again. But David didn't let a potentially flawed perspective on the nature of God overcome his need to pray and plead for God's loving and gracious nature to intercede.

Stop reading these words and rest your mind on that last sentence for a moment. Maybe you're attempting to stay aloof and detached from God because the shame of coming into His presence to confess your wrongdoings causes a measure of spiritual paralysis. In these agonizing hours our hearts cast a veil over the nature of God and how He treats those who come to Him in remorse and repentance.

King David felt this, too. The real agony for him was in suspecting that he might be removed from the all-permeating radiance of God's presence. So he comes humbly before the Lord and acknowledges the agony he has thrust himself into. And in that torment, five important words come pouring from David's lips: *create*, *renew*, *cast*, *restore*, and *uphold*.

Only God had both the divinity and the desire to create a clean heart in the chasm of David's sin-ravaged spirit. In the same way God created the world by the power of His divine word, He would need to declare David's heart clean again. If only God was willing! And He was! He is. Only God possessed the righteousness to *renew* a right spirit in David. Only God had the love and compassion to not *cast* David away from His presence. Only a God who embodied joy in and of Himself could *restore* the joy of salvation to David's dull and diminishing soul. Only God possessed the kind of compassionate spirit to heal David's broken spirit after his egregious sin.

What does David possess here that we so often lack? Nothing but a heart that had been burst open like spring flowers to receive the gospel-drenched sunlight that leads to unrestrained confession.

Do you feel cast away from God's presence this Christmas season? It is easy to feel that way when your sins have created vast barriers between you and God. David shows us that there is a way back before the ball drops on the New Year. The God of all creation can also create new hearts for His created beings. So as the bright lights of Christmas cast their shimmering glow on the artificial contrivances of this idealized holiday, the brighter heart of Jesus serves as a laser advancing toward the remote regions of your heart with undimmed love. And in the desolate places where your barely hidden offenses feel barren and disrobed before the eyes of a holy God, take courage because a repentant heart is the occasion for the Creator to do some joyous re-creating.

> If we confess our sins, he is faithful and just to forgive us our sins and to cleanse us from all unrighteousness. (1 John 1:9)

Reconnect with your Creator, who grants clean hearts and renewed spirits to all who confess their sins with godly sorrow and remorse.

May the Lord *create*, *renew*, *cast*, *restore*, and *uphold* you today.

PAUSE, PONDER, AND PRAY

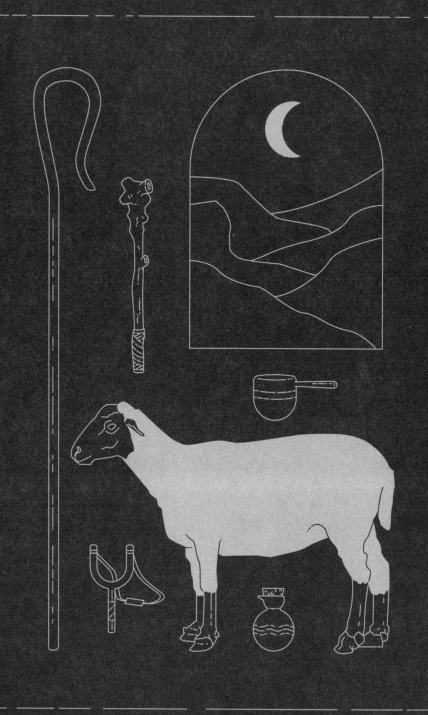

EVEN THOUGH

Even though I walk through the valley of the shadow of
death, I will fear no evil, for you are with me; your rod and
your staff, they comfort me.
PSALM 23:4

*E*ven though . . .
Let those two words just hang there for a moment. What kind of imagery do they evoke as they search the inner reaches of your consciousness? If you find commonality with David, they likely provide a distressing realism, which is that shadowy, deathly valleys are a stark inevitability for the man or woman of faith. Thankfully for both David and us, these undesirable passageways don't end in perpetual isolation and unresolved despair.

David tells us what he does with this familiar fear that infiltrates his troubled soul like an invisible phantom. He declares, without a trace of faux masculinity, that he will *fear no evil*. Refreshingly, he isn't throwing down any sort of macho-driven bravado here, though if anyone possessed the qualifications, it would have been David. We remember how he wrestled untamed lions with his bare hands, took down Goliath the giant with a mere slingshot, and slayed tens of thousands of his greatest enemies with a ferocity that became the stuff of legend. Able hands, fatal weapons, and magnificent armies were all things David possessed and could employ with the skill of a talented and seasoned warrior. But shadowy, deathly valleys? That's another story entirely. Whatever skill he carried with him on the battlefield, he would have none of it as he roamed through bouts of shudder-inducing dread and disheartening solitude.

I wonder what kind of shadowy valleys you have wandered through over the course of the past twelve months? Maybe your valley has been an unexpected physical ailment or some relational unrest with a loved one that has propelled you into a state of anxiety you can't seem to rid yourself of, no matter what kind of medication you've tried. It could be that you've been sinned against through some crooked form of gossip or slander, and you feel like your once-good name has been permanently tarnished. Events like these may have thrust you into ever-evolving battles with bitterness that culminate with prayers such as "I didn't ask for any of this" repeatedly flying from your lips. You wonder why God thought it a good idea to allow you to walk through this unexplained season of trial and suffering.

So let me pose another question which I'll follow with a short thought. When do you most sense your need for God? Is it in the exuberance you experience after a series of fortunate events has befallen you—that career advancement, salary increase, relationship development, goal achievement, or a realized dream? Or is it in those ominous instances where it feels like all the color that exists in the world has been drained out and you have been relegated to a secluded corner in the lowlands of life? I'll ask again, *in which of those two scenarios do you most sense your need for God?* I'm going to take a stab in the dark and go with the latter. But the most important realization to emerge from your experience in these shadowy valleys will be what David so winsomely describes:

> For you are with me; your rod and your staff, they
> comfort me.

Would you mind pausing for just a moment to reflect on the simple profundity of those words? What might God be bringing to mind in the buried deeps of your core? For David, it was an undeniable presence that he had to sing and speak out loud in order to remind himself of the source of his comfort.

I remember one summer my parents sent me and my younger brother Jason to a church camp in this idyllic mountain setting, surrounded by glistening blue lakes and forests of pine-scented greenery. Upon arrival, I could not shake a debilitating homesickness. My longing to be back home cast me into a state of despair so profound that even the camp counselors failed in their admirable attempts to console me. I craved the safety, comfort, and familiarity my parents provided.

I can recall one afternoon when I was hiding away in my room, the bedroom door creaked open and in walked my brother Jason who, without a word, sat down next to me. In a moment of unforgettable tenderness, he put his hand on my back and told me that everything was going to be okay. With simple words and a soothing touch for the saddened heart of a homesick boy.

But here's what hits home for me now: I would have never needed the comfort of my brother's heart-formed hand had I not been in such a dark and discomforting place. Jason reminded me that it would not be too long before we'd be back with our parents in the familiar surroundings of home. He reminded me of what I had to hope for in the confines of an unhopeful place.

Like He did for David, God ordains the valleys so that our lips may form the words "even though." In the downcastness of our dimmest days, He promises to be near to us in the nothingness and faithful in the forlornness. Even though shadowy valleys will make up many chapters in the story of your life, you are always safe to hope again.

Because He is with you.

PAUSE, PONDER, AND PRAY

ALWAYS

"And behold, I am with you always, to the end of the age."
MATTHEW 28:20

F or many of us, there are few things that cause as much sadness as goodbyes. I remember when we relocated to Ohio for a ministry call back in 2010. If only you could have seen the sad, sorry faces painted all over me, my wife, our teenage daughter, and two unhappy cats on the day we left the only home we had ever known for the new frontiers of Northeast Ohio.

To give you some context, I was born and raised in sunny Southern California, so this move meant I was leaving behind most of my family, close friends, and familiar places that had formed me for the better part of four decades. I will never forget the almost unbearable feeling of loss that hovered over me like a fog during our final few days of farewells. I was barely able to get through even the most casual conversation without my eyes turning into a stream of ugly, uncontrollable tears. There was a sense of finality to this goodbye, which is why I think I felt completely enveloped by it. The emotions were erratic and complex because I knew there would be no coming back from the journey we were about to embark on.

I've often wondered if this is similar (in some ways) to what the disciples experienced as Jesus prepared for His ascent to heaven. As He gave instructions for the good work He was leaving His friends to accomplish in His physical absence, how deeply were they affected by feelings of loss and heartbreak? Imagine all the hours spent with Jesus traveling through towns and cities where they ministered to the crowds, shared the gospel, healed the sick, and fed the hungry. Imagine all the myriad moments in between that aren't even recorded in the gospel accounts. Walking together down dusty, unpaved roads, gathering around the fire to stay warm on chilly nights, sharing stories from their childhoods, making silly jokes about inconsequential things, and experiencing hours of profound vulnerability as they contemplated a future they had all guessed so wrongly about.

How were these men feeling as Jesus prepared for His divine departure? Well, we know for sure that Jesus knew how they felt because He didn't leave them with a detailed instruction manual to tuck away in their backpacks. Instead, He talked about His proximity to them as they began a death-defying work that would take the world by storm like no other. Notice the phrasing. He would be with them . . . *always*. Meaning, *forevermore*, *eternally*, *perpetually*, and every other word that describes what it means to never be absent or alone.

And it feels both poetic and paramount the way Jesus adds *to the end of the age*. In other words, the nearness of Jesus would be as immeasurable as the universe if one were to try to calculate it ever coming to an end. Like the existence of matter itself, there would never be a single second, minute, hour, or epoch when Jesus would *not* be present with His friends. And we know that these words traveled even further than the ears of His twelve disciples because we are His friends, too.

He said, *Behold, I am with you always.* Look, observe, take notice, don't miss, and stand back in awe at the enormity of what I'm saying.

In other words, open your eyes wide and see that my presence will not be like a flickering candle that invariably grows dim, burns out, and needs to be replaced. It's not like an electronic device whose batteries begin to slowly run down the minute you turn it on. It's not like a car running low on fuel that begins to cough and sputter when the needle drops too far beneath the E. It's not like the broken promise of someone who pledged to be faithful but sadly lost interest in staying true.

The presence of Jesus is more akin to the fixture of the sun. As long as you live, you will never know a day when the sun is not settled in space and glowing like the perpetual orange orb that it is. Sure, clouds will emerge to obscure the immensity of its light, and rain will fall to lessen the magnitude of its warmth, but the sun will never cease to provide the blazing hotness of its blinding glow.

And yet, even this metaphor eventually breaks down because the sun is a created object that has no guarantee of everlasting light and warmth. The sun is not the Son. The Son is a light that will retain its brightness forever, beyond the end of all earthly and universal ages.

What Jesus offered His twelve disciples is a gift that extends to every disciple since His ascension. Do you need to remember this timeless truth anew, as all the lights, tinsel, and ornaments that surround you present a yearly reminder that even the loveliest things of this world will eventually be turned off, taken down, and stored away in forgotten silence? Do you need to remember that Jesus is the one person who never ceases to exist in all the known and unknown corners of your life in the New Year? Do you need to remember that "though the earth gives way, though the mountains be moved into the heart of the sea, though its waters roar and foam, though the mountains tremble at its swelling" (Ps. 46:2–3), He is *with you always, to the end of the age?*

Remember this promise that Jesus will never forget to keep.

PAUSE, PONDER, AND PRAY

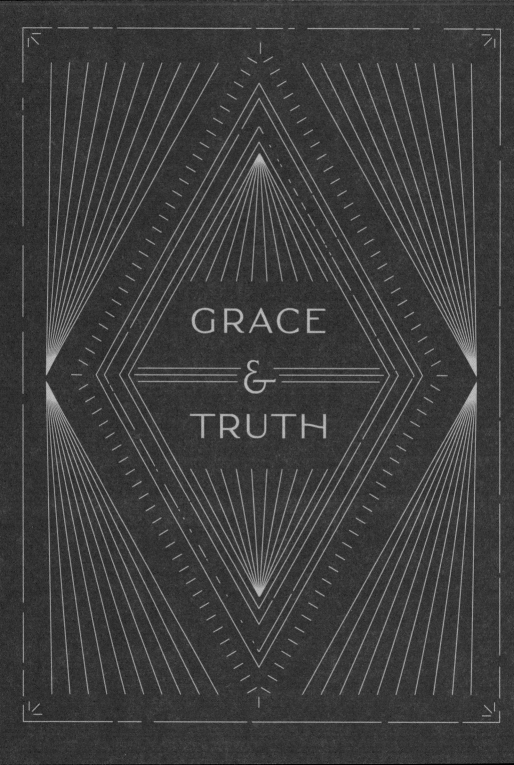

GRACE
&
TRUTH

AMONG US

*And the Word became flesh and dwelt among us, and
we have seen his glory, glory as of the only Son from the
Father, full of grace and truth.*
JOHN 1:14

If you had to summarize the message of Christmas in one sentence, you might say it like this: *God became flesh and dwelt among us.* If you've spent any amount of time in church circles, those words can easily and tragically pass through you like rays of sun through curtainless windows. Except we need these words to pierce us, not merely pass through us. The One who said "light," and light suddenly appeared is the same One who became a man and lived among us, died in place of us, and rose from the grave to be our only hope of having peace with a holy God.

It is no surprise that Christmastime comes to us year after year in the artificial sparkle of the silver, gold, glitter, and gifts that highlight the spectacle of the season. Many of us remember the magical traditions our parents created for us with fondness and nostalgia: trimming the perfect Christmas tree, toiling over Christmas wish lists, baking an innumerable assortment of sugar cookies, making gingerbread houses that collapsed within minutes of completion, sledding for hours in lush, powdery snow, and watching favorite holiday TV programs around the fire. You won't hear me knocking these kinds of memories in the slightest! I carry them all myself and do my best to recreate them every year in the spirit of the season.

But these memories, as good as they can be, don't capture what is being spoken to us in the first chapter of John's Gospel.

And the Word became flesh and dwelt among us.

Let your imagination rest on these words for a moment. I've heard it said that in this life we will never be able to adequately comprehend the magnitude of this statement: that Jesus humbled Himself, became flesh, and willingly gave Himself to be the atoning sacrifice for our sins as He condescended from the lofty abodes of heaven to the humble soil of the earth. The apostle John is giving testimony to the most remarkable of miracles here, which is that the Creator of the universe became like one of His created beings so that all those God chose to save wouldn't have to live separated from Him for all eternity. The idea that the Son of God, the Creator of all created things, broke into the universe to dwell with His rebellious creatures is a truth so significant that the transformation of our souls depends on our belief in it.

Imagine wanting to draw near to those who wanted nothing more than to get as far away from you as possible? In our lives, we might determine that the healthiest solution for those who have become our adversaries is to create as much space as possible between us and them. And this can be for many good reasons: we have reached a point of incompatibility, and our sense of spiritual and emotional peace depends on the healthy distance we can maintain. Fair enough. But then there's Jesus, who clothed Himself with human flesh so that we might not be clothed in our sin. Think of the kind of selfless heart that would do what Jesus so charitably did. Think of the Creator of the universe, the Ruler of the earth, and the Shepherd of your soul being this unashamedly affectionate for *you*, of all people, with a love so full of grace and truth that your only response when confronted with His majesty is to declare "GLORY!"

The voice of the Lord makes the deer give birth and strips the forests bare, and in his temple all cry, "Glory!" The Lord sits enthroned over the flood; the Lord sits enthroned as king forever. (Ps. 29:9–10)

It's true that we have not seen the glory of Christ the way John and the other disciples were able to see it in the flesh two thousand years ago. We read the gospel accounts and can only imagine what it must have been like to be face-to-face with the Creator and Redeemer of the universe. And yet elsewhere in John's Gospel, Jesus also says, "Blessed are those who have not seen and yet have believed" (John 20:29). The love of God that "has been poured into our hearts through the Holy Spirit" (Rom. 5:5) is something more astoundingly significant than if we had been there in the flesh with Jesus Himself. Because Jesus ascended to the right hand of the Father, we enjoy His personal presence through the indwelling of the Holy Spirit, which encourages our hearts and increases our faith in ways we will need to enter glory to even begin to grasp.

We have seen his glory.

We would do well in this wonderful season to drink in the wonder of this astonishing passage in light of our entrance into a new year already full of uncharted physical and spiritual destinations that we are still in the dark about. To remember that the Word made flesh who came to *dwell among us* has a voice that carries a weight of transcendent life force and beauty. The Father who sits enthroned in heaven sent the Son who sits enthroned at His right hand to uphold us by His lovely nail-pierced hands. In the same way that you can't exist without flesh on your bones, Jesus remains closer to you than even your own flesh. Take good comfort that the One who came to dwell among you is the One who will not desert you on January 1.

He is among us.

PAUSE, PONDER, AND PRAY

IT IS
GOOD
to be
NEAR
GOD

Psalm 73:28

GOD TO BE NEAR

But for me it is good to be near God; I have made the Lord
GOD my refuge, that I may tell of all your works.
PSALM 73:28

This wonderfully tuneful song written by Asaph the psalmist reads like a man singing to us from the melodic overflow of his joyful heart about the goodness of God's nearness. Asaph understands the significance of being near to God and that His nearness *to us* flows from His heart *for us*.

"It was so good!" is something we tell people when they ask us how we experienced something enjoyable or meaningful. The concert was *so good*. That new restaurant was *so good*. The time we spent with friends over the weekend was *so good*. The movie we saw, the book we read, the album we listened to was *so good*. Each one of these good experiences reflects an expectation that was met by our senses in the most pleasurable of ways.

We know when things are good because we are able to compare them with things that have been less than good. This can also be applied to the condition of our heart and to the kinds of things we have let near to it that are of less than good quality. Eventually, this kind of subtle yet lethal fruit we consume produces spiritual fruit that ends up consuming us. Read the story of Adam and Eve in Genesis 3 for a more descriptive rendering of what I'm describing.

With that said, would you read slowly and reflect on these two incredibly vulnerable verses from Asaph?

> When my soul was embittered, when I was pricked
> in heart, I was brutish and ignorant; I was like a beast
> toward you. (Ps. 73:21–22)

Like most songwriters, Asaph is wonderfully self-reflective, which means he also possesses one of the fruits of self-reflection: an ever-increasing knowledge of self. What Asaph is experiencing in these verses is the plight of the human condition—that we have the tendency to return the grace and mercy of God with grumbling mouths and malcontent hearts. At times, we treat God the way we are treated by animals, who lack the depth of character to appreciate the ways we care for and nurture them. We become bitter and resentful when we feel like God is falling short in His obligations to cater to our every whim. Asaph recognizes this colossal defect of his heart but doesn't allow it to create distance from or resistance to God. And it is not for nothing either. His nearness to God provides opportunities to be a spokesman on behalf of God's good works. God's presence becomes the place where he finds his refuge, and this compels him to be a musical ambassador to the glory of that reality.

In general, we human beings tend to be champion-level drifters. Even the good things and great people God places around us need to be pursued with intentionality, or we will wander away from them like tumbleweeds in a windstorm. We are prone to complacency, to taking people for granted and pulling away from them much more than we push toward them. But God wants us to have hearts that increasingly long for the goodness that comes with being near to Him and then adopting intentional practices to stay there—not only for our good but for the benefit of others as well. It is for the purpose of boasting to others about the goodness of God's nearness that God draws near to us even when we are at our most reserved and remote.

As the Christmas season unfolds and the New Year looms on the horizon, you can probably think of something in the near future that feels daunting and may even surface some dispiriting weight of worry and alienation. Perhaps you feel like no one is near enough to respond with care and love to the unsettledness of your soul. Listen to the song of Asaph the psalmist. The nearness of God was a refuge to him that caused his lips to form words of praise around the amazing works God had done. Knowing that the Lord was near gave him the reassurance to pursue the only refuge that could provide safety, strength, and solace when all the world was collapsing around him.

It is good to be near God.

May the song of your heart move toward the surest of all havens.

PAUSE, PONDER, AND PRAY

MAKE OUR HOME

Jesus answered him, "If anyone loves me, he will keep my
word, and my Father will love him, and we will come to
him and make our home with him."
JOHN 14:23

If you are like me, you love to be home, especially during the holidays, because home is the place we feel most at ease with ourselves and our surroundings. It is the place where we can truly be ourselves, without needing to feel the pressure to perform or put on a persona. I understand that not everyone feels this way, but I love to entertain, especially when the holiday season is in full bloom. Nothing is as festive as bustling around a decorated house while the smells of sugary and savory food marinate the air. What I look forward to most is when close friends arrive and they waste no time making themselves right at home. They know that our home is their home so they don't ask permission to enjoy what we've already declared is theirs. This kind of familiarity brings me joy because it's a testimony to the kind of closeness that has been cultivated in our relationship.

Whether we care to admit it or not, this is probably how we would all love our homes to feel during this season, which is the reason Christmas is portrayed in books, magazines, postcards, and movie scenes as a living room filled with warm fires, cheerful lights, colorful gifts, and family members enjoying the inviting comforts of home. But obviously, this Currier and Ives vision of Christmastime rarely aligns with our experiences.

We know this because home can be a predicament during the holidays. Relationships that are in varying states of turmoil have to all come together on this one special day to allegedly celebrate peace on earth and goodwill toward men (Luke 2:14). For many of us, this phrase feels like nothing more than an idealistic sentiment that only becomes true at the end of Hallmark Channel Christmas specials. In reality, what we know as "home" can dash our expectations every holiday season because the relationships required to comprise a healthy home remain unrepaired and broken beyond belief. Maybe this is what the holidays have become for you, so it's understandable how difficult it is to imagine the concept of "home" being something that evokes feelings of invitation and warmth.

Is it hard for you to imagine the Father, Son, and Holy Spirit choosing to make their home with you? If I'm being honest, and there's no reason to lie, I think it is for me, too. I don't have to wander too far into the caverns of my soul to find patches of fear, guilt, and shame sprouting up through the soil. Sometimes it's impossible to imagine anyone wanting to be within a hundred miles of me, much less make their home with me. Thank God I am not God! So deep are His mercy, grace, love, and compassion that the moment we are redeemed from our sins, we become a place for the triune God to love us, remain with us, and make His home with us forever.

Whether this season has been characterized by excitable smiles or worrisome sighs, would you read that short passage at the top of the page again? Jesus is responding to a question from Judas Iscariot, His friend, disciple, and eventual betrayer. Jesus desired Judas to understand that the kind of home he lacked but longed for was within his grasp if his love could only be reordered and renewed. Sadly, Judas allowed his heart to seek comfort from the heartless clang of silver coins. I wonder if this exchange between Jesus and Judas hints at some of the "homes" you have attempted to construct in order to try to satisfy a familial longing that has been lacking in your own life?

So, what does this mean for you then? Well, it means that wherever you are, God is there with you in the most familiar, most welcoming, most intimate way imaginable. It means you are the place God desires to be, since you are now His offspring and heir to the riches of His grace. It means that before Christ saved you, you were like an orphan, but now you have been adopted into a family that comes with a Father who has made His home with you and His Son who is preparing a home for you on that day when "he will wipe away every tear from their eyes, and death shall be no more, neither shall there be mourning, nor crying, nor pain anymore, for the former things have passed away" (Rev. 21:4).

The home God has is with you.

PAUSE, PONDER, AND PRAY

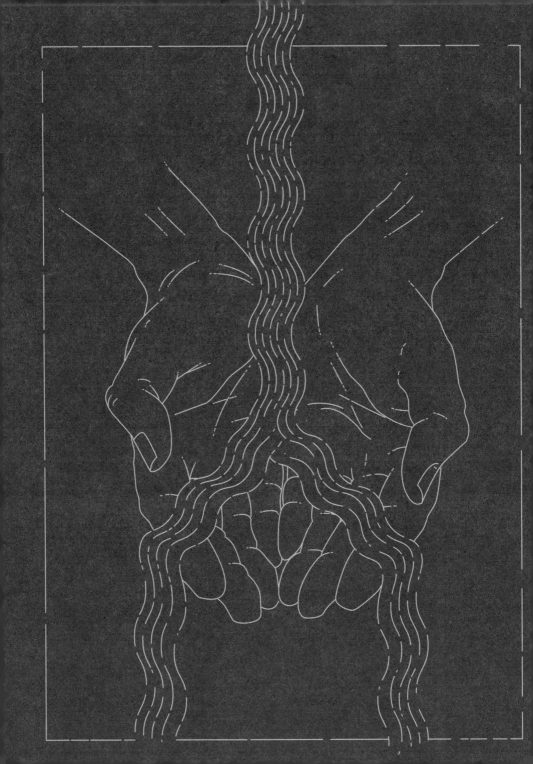

DRAW NEAR

Draw near to God, and he will draw near to you.
Cleanse your hands, you sinners, and purify your hearts,
you double-minded.
JAMES 4:8

We probably all know a person in our life who doesn't mind "tell-ing it like it is." If you don't know someone like that, well, you may be that person! You know—the person who doesn't choose their words so carefully, refuses to beat around the bush, and is transparent about who they are and exactly what they think. Of course, these same people usually possess the unenviable power to create awkward silences and conversational eruptions while everyone else is on their best behavior. They are also in perpetual danger of offending everyone they come in contact with and scaring everyone off in the process. It probably doesn't help that the social situations we find ourselves in at Christmastime bring us into contact with these personality types more often than at any other time of the year.

Interestingly, you get a sense of this from James, the half brother of Jesus, who feels like that friend or family member who has zero problem with "saying it like it is," regardless of the situation. Could it be that James shows us that bluntness can be next to godliness if it is driven by the kindness of Christ? I'll leave it right there.

What our friend James is doing, under the inspiration of the Holy Spirit, is issuing a warning against worldliness as He writes to Jewish Christians who are suffering persecution from those who are unhappy about their conversion to Christianity. Because of this, some of these believers would have been tempted to partake in worldly activities to avoid the suffering they were experiencing as Christians.

Sometimes, when we are experiencing resistance to our faith in some unique capacity, our first thought might be to stop being so bold and instead to cozy up to the world in such a way that nobody will be any the wiser that we are followers of Christ. And given the polarization that has characterized so many pockets of our lives in recent years, it is understandable to be concerned about how people might perceive us on any number of issues.

What is interesting is the manner in which James encourages these suffering but struggling people: *draw near to God, and he will draw near to you*. The cure for worldliness is not only to cease from doing worldly things. I mean, to stop doing worldly things and then become smug and pompous for not doing those things would in fact be another form of worldliness! But drawing near to God is an act of humility that requires a spiritual cleansing and purification that only God can work in and through you. But the first step comes by simply drawing near to God. Going to Him with all your worldly stains and asking to be washed clean of your unrighteousness.

In case we think drawing near to God is something we should just do whenever we get around to it, James communicates his words with a sense of candid urgency. "Cleanse your hands and purify your hearts you bunch of double-minded sinners!" James is saying that the time for drawing near to God is *now*. Most preachers would be a little hesitant in bringing that much force to bear on their congregations, but James gets right down to it. And some might choose to interpret it as overly harsh and intense if it wasn't preceded by one of the most hopeful promises contained in all of Scripture:

Draw near to God, and he will draw near to you.

Does this feel like the last thing you want to engage in at this season of the year? It can be so difficult to look back on the past twelve months and see areas where your life has become more deeply conformed to the feelings, desires, ambitions, and opinions of the world. Doing some internal inventory of the soul will likely reveal some patterns in your life that need to be addressed and repented of. Thankfully, this is the place where the Spirit of God does His most gracious excavation work because He wants to create a heart that has the kind of soil His fruit can best grow in. Clean hands and pure hearts are the Christ-cleansing work that happens so that God and mankind can draw near to each other once again.

Draw near to God.

Remember who is drawing near to you in your far away-ness because it is the One who has said, "All that the Father gives me will come to me, and whoever comes to me I will never cast out" (John 6:37). Draw near to the One who drew near to you first, who chose you before the foundation of the world to purify you and cleanse you from a heart that leads to dirty hands and double-mindedness.

Draw near to the One who is already near to you.

PAUSE, PONDER, AND PRAY

WHERE SHALL I GO?

Where shall I go from your Spirit? Or where shall I flee
from your presence? If I ascend to heaven, you are there! If I
make my bed in Sheol, you are there!

PSALM 139:7–8

An odd thing that became a good thing for my wife many years ago was the advent (no pun) of texting. I know, most people go on and on about how society has lost the art of engaging in real-life conversations since all we seem to do now is text back and forth with our lifeless digital devices. On one level, it's hard to disagree with that sentiment. Relationships are always going to benefit most from face-to-face contact where we can read each other's facial expressions, hear the tone in our voices, read a person's body language, and acquire the kind of social manners that are best developed through human contact.

To be clear, texting can never replace the physicality of flesh-and-blood community. And yet none of us have the privilege of spending every waking hour with our friends and loved ones, as lovely as that would be for the flourishing of our relationships. One considerable thing texting has done is allow me and my wife to be in constant conversation with each other when we would otherwise be out of contact altogether. At any given moment, we are a message away from asking how the other person is doing, seeing what they are up to, clicking off some encouraging words, and knowing how we can pray.

I'm telling you, it's not all bad! In fact, I'll go as far to say that it is an imperfect picture of the kind of relationship we have with our Father in heaven.

In one of the most beautiful songs ever written, King David makes the argument that he cannot escape the presence of God, no matter where he goes. Like Jonah, David finds that there is no place in the universe too remote for God's Spirit to exist. Unlike Jonah, this is an enormous comfort to David, as he considers the intimacy God cultivates with His people. In this life, we have no hope of ever escaping God, and only our guilt and shame create in us the aspirations to do so.

The Christmas season provides ample opportunities for "fleeing from" one thing and "ascending to" another. For one month out of the calendar year (unless you're one of those early adopters who begins decorating the day after Halloween—we should talk), we can use holiday distractions to make all the humdrum hardships of our lives disappear for a hot minute. We can even attempt to keep God at bay while reserving January 1 to be the day we enter back into His good graces by getting our behavior back on track. There's a heartbreaking sort of silliness to it all, like when children think they can do something that's going to escape the notice of their parents, but it couldn't be more ridiculous or less clever in its flabby execution. When we begin to comprehend the grace of God, and how wide His arms are to embrace the repentant, we will say, "Where shall I go from your Spirit?" like it's a good thing.

As we consider the incarnation of Immanuel, whose name means "God with us," will we find our greatest comfort in knowing that whatever places and spaces the New Year brings us to geographically or otherwise, we can have the confidence that God is with us before, during, and after our arrival. Like David, we can approach God with the exhilaration that we are known by Him with a degree of intimacy unknown anywhere else.

> O LORD, you have searched me and known me! You know when I sit down and when I rise up; you discern my thoughts from afar. You search out my path and my lying down and are acquainted with all my ways. Even before a word is on my tongue, behold, O LORD, you know it altogether. You hem me in, behind and before, and lay your hand upon me. Such knowledge is too wonderful for me; it is high; I cannot attain it. (Ps. 139:1–6)

Of course, this intense degree of intimacy would be terrifying if God wasn't famous for abounding in steadfast love, faithfulness, mercy, grace, and abated anger. Because these character qualities exist, we not only marvel at the wonder of it, but we also invite Him to search us this deeply over and over again.

> Search me, O God, and know my heart! Try me and know my thoughts! And see if there be any grievous way in me, and lead me in the way everlasting! (Ps. 139:23–24)

The way everlasting is the way of Jesus. A knowledge too wonderful for us so that the grievous ways in us would be met with the gracious ways of Jesus, which is how God stooped low to us in order to search us, know us, and never leave us without the help and hope we need.

Where shall you go?

PAUSE, PONDER, AND PRAY

ADVENT DAY 19

YOUR FACE DO I SEEK

*Hear, O Lord, when I cry aloud; be gracious to me and
answer me! You have said, "Seek my face." My heart says to
you, "Your face, Lord, do I seek."*

PSALM 27:7–8

A common goal today in our post-Christian world is the acquisition of power. I don't mean the kind of power that seeks to control and dominate over other people (there's plenty of that too, sadly). I'm talking about some good old-fashioned electricity, specifically when your cell phone is down to 1 percent, and you are seconds away from being cut off from all communication to the natural world. What do we do? We scramble about like lost children in an amusement park to find an electrical outlet because a fully charged cell phone is the only way for us to stay connected to the world.

Our pursuit of power goes deeper than this, though. We are all seeking numerous sources to power the many angles contained in achieving the ambitions of our existence. For example, some of us seek money as the power source for accomplishing our dreams, so we plug into our life's work at an unsustainable pace to generate the dollars necessary for our dreams to materialize. We are all seekers, and by seekers I don't mean esoteric New Agers on a mystical quest to discover the meaning of life. What I mean is—okay, maybe I do mean that, because all of the ways we seek power to connect, control, achieve, and accomplish are deeply attached to our belief in the meaning of life and the power we believe it has to deliver us happiness and hope.

Psalm 27 is a song about David's needing the most secure and trusted power source available. He is crying out and complaining loudly, "Lord, please hear me!" You can feel the gravity of his angst as he sings these sorrowful words. This is a man after God's own heart who is pleading with the heart of God. Curiously, he doesn't feel the need to be polite, monitor his tone, or be extra careful with his words. David has written this chorus before and many times after. He understands that God is the power source for everything he needs to endure the predicament he finds himself in. So, what does David need exactly? He needs what we all need when we find ourselves in the throes of depleted power sources: the face of God.

So many things jockey for our devotion in the nerve endings of life. For some, it's that one click on the computer, food in the fridge, binging on Netflix, or any one of the endless supply of mind-numbing exercises that seek to alleviate our stress but ultimately fail because they can't hear, they can't answer, and they don't care. David's heart was moved differently, but let us not imagine that he didn't face the same temptations we do. His earth-shattering sins with Bathsheba and Uriah tell a different story.

I wonder how this moves you today? Do you wish you had the courage to cry aloud to God like David did, without feeling timid or encumbered? Is there something in your life that has brought your stress level to a place that nothing else on earth seems to be able to relieve any longer? What would God have us do in moments like this?

You have said, "Seek my face."

What does this mean exactly, to seek the face of God? To put it simply, it means that before all the other things in our life that are clamoring for our attention and devotion, we pursue Christ. It means we acknowledge "for all that is in the world—the desires of the flesh and the desires of the eyes and pride of life—is not from the Father but is from the world" (1 John 2:16). See, there is never a moment when we are not pursuing something or someone for what we consider to be the betterment of ourselves. Our souls were created for worship, to be given over to something we consider praiseworthy. Our heart defaults to seeking a vast multitude of faces that do nothing other than threaten to capture our affections—affections we should reserve for one face. Obviously, this does not mean we don't seek other faces that God has placed in our lives for our blessing and flourishing. It means that as we seek these other faces, we guard against them becoming gods by always seeking the face of God before all others.

Imagine the blessings in store for you if you spent this Christmas season taking inventory of all the pursuits that may have become poisonous for you. Some may be subtle, barely detectable. Others may be glaring and overt and embarrassingly obvious. But the one thing they will all have in common is the passion they steal from your heart that is the sole property of Christ alone. Imagine what will happen if you seek His face above all other faces.

My heart says to you, "Your face, LORD, do I seek."

May we go once again to the source of who will hear our prayers and answer our dilemmas. May our hearts long to gaze into the face of God and to be known and assured by the warmth of His words.

Seek the gracious light of God's face.

PAUSE, PONDER, AND PRAY

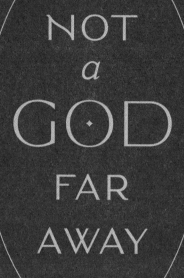

NOT
a
GOD
FAR
AWAY

NOT A GOD FAR AWAY

*"Am I a God who is only near"—this is the LORD's
declaration—"and not a God who is far away?"*
JEREMIAH 23:23 CSB

It's always a matter of dispute whether long-distance relationships have the ability to "work." Regardless of whether they are of a romantic nature or not, we struggle to maintain close relationships with people we cannot be with in the flesh. Of course, technology has helped with this, as Zoom, Skype, and FaceTime have made long-distance connections much more personal. But as much as we are thankful to have that ability to see people as we are talking to them, it still pales in comparison to being in the same place as them.

Christmas Day 2020 is not a day I'll soon forget. In a "normal" year, our daughter and extended family will fly in from out of state and join us for a week of Christmas festivities filled with all of the classic Christmassy things you can imagine. Our house becomes a wonderland of delicious food, favorite games, holiday movies, and nonstop yuletide tunes. My wife Melissa and I look forward to this coveted week all year long! But when December 2020 finally came, nobody was able to come for Christmas due to a spike in COVID outbreaks that began right after Thanksgiving. As the season of togetherness drew closer, it became a season of far-awayness for us and many others.

Throughout Scripture, God reassures His people that He is not a God who is far away. Even though He is not with us currently in the flesh, He wants us to know that the presence He provides for us through the indwelling of the Holy Spirit is even closer than if Jesus Christ were here in the flesh. How easily we forget that God is not a God far away! He is not like the ancient Greek gods who dwelled high in the clouds or the lofty mountains and remained distant, aloof, and angry with the people who called upon them.

In a sense, God wants us to embrace the absurdity that He is a God that keeps a cool distance, or locks Himself away in some unreachable black hole in the cosmos. God is at hand, but His hands are never immobile like the hands on a broken clock. God is near, but His nearness is not like a light bulb whose luminescence is dependent on the strength of the currents responsible for powering it. God is a listener, but His ears are never distracted by the volume of words that float toward the stars and fill up the ether. His Spirit indwells every corner of the spheres as well as every square inch of our souls.

Sometimes our sin or our circumstances can make us feel like God is being distant with us. Like He turns the ringer off on His cell phone, sets up an out-of-office reply on His email, or travels to a remote corner of the universe for an extended vacation. But God is always at hand. Always at the ready. A God who stays awake while we're sleeping. A God who is upholding us when our knees buckle underneath us. A God who can't be far away because the closeness He has with His creatures is one of His unfailing attributes. This is no long-distance relationship. In fact, it is closer than the closest relationship you will ever have on this earth.

What is interesting about this passage in Jeremiah is that it is spoken to prophets who were speaking lies. God declared that He was against these men. And that is great hope for us living in times where at times it seems like God isn't interested in dealing with those who use His name to spread lies and untruths. In reality God sees. He is as close in judgment to those who are unjustly representing Him as He is in friendship to those who are faithful to Him.

Maybe this feels like a season of far awayness for you. Maybe friends and family are physically close, but you can't shake this spirit of solitude and loneliness that hangs like a mist suspended in mid-air all around you. If only it was unusual, but it sadly and encouragingly isn't. We remember the night before Christ's death. How He pleaded with His slumbering friends to remain watchful with Him as sleep cast its untimely spell over their tired eyes. Sometimes, the people who are closest to us are farthest from us. How did Jesus respond? By going back to His Father who is never far away.

This reminds us that unlike the Greek gods of old, who came from the vain imaginations of men, the true and living God is not an oblivious deity. He will repay evil; He will enact justice. He will bless the righteous. He will uphold the weak and weary who have trusted in His name. He will never be far from those who move in closer to the place where He already is and will forever be.

Bring Him your unspoken words that feel too heavy to utter to another living soul. Bring Him the disappointing people, the discouraging moments, the disheartening news, and the distance all of this has created between you and Him, your Creator.

He is not a God far away.

PAUSE, PONDER, AND PRAY

THE LORD IS NOT SLOW

The Lord is not slow to fulfill his promise as some count slowness, but is patient toward you, not wishing that any should perish, but that all should reach repentance.

2 PETER 3:9

We live in such a fast-moving society, don't we? We are likely experiencing that to its fullest right now during the Christmas season. Going shopping can be such a mad rush as we dash in and out of stores at a manic pace, wearing out our poor ATM cards, ever aware of the money we are spending and the time we are lacking to complete all our tasks on time. The holiday season tests our patience, too. We want things now, and if shopping isn't our thing, Amazon Prime is right there to ship us what we need overnight. Amazon is, in fact, not slow to fulfill its promise of free shipping and overnight service. Unfortunately, this is how we count slowness. Something that doesn't happen or arrive exactly as fast as we desire it to. We don't want Amazon to be patient toward us, as much as we usually don't want God to be patient with anyone else but us.

But God, in all of His perceived slowness, is actually patient toward you. And them. Think of it like this: if it is in the heart of God to draw close to His hell-bound creatures, then it means He will be patient toward those whose paths have not yet been rerouted.

How do you count slowness when it comes to your view of how God acts in the affairs of humanity? If you were honest, could you say that you lack patience with God's pacing? Are there people you'd like to see come to justice? Are there relationships you wish could be resolved? Are there loved ones long gone that you want to be reunited with? Are there family members far from God that you wish He would finally intervene and save?

By the way, none of those desires are wrong. We rightly desire justice, restored relationships, and lost family members to come to know Christ. What we need to remember is that God in His sovereignty has a particular purpose that He is unfolding with a timing we don't have the mental capacity to understand. Why does God wait? We're going to have to wait to know the answer to that question. What we do know is that the hand of God is only slow inasmuch as His heart is patiently seeking to save the lost.

> And now, O Lord, for what do I wait? My hope is in you. (Ps. 39:7)

Waiting for the ultimate fulfillment of God's promises keeps us hoping for what we cannot see. We never hope for what we already have! We don't need to have patience for something we have already received! God makes us wait for those very reasons, so that hope and patience produce a character that brings about the joy and happiness of Christ in us. God is not slow like we define slowness. In the same way you are able to wait for Christmas morning much better than a child because the waiting and anticipating are as much a part of the joy as the receiving, God wants you to know a joy that can only come through a patient heart immersed in the surety of hope.

Years ago, I had a pretty significant falling out with a pastor colleague of mine. Our relationship ended in a heap of ruins that looked like the equivalent of a multi-car pileup. It was a horrific sight to see and one that brought many nights of sleepless despair as I prayed to God to help me make sense of the nonsensical way that everything had disintegrated. Years passed, and little changed, but I was still faced with subtle, if not constant reminders—social media posts and small talk with his acquaintances, to awkward interactions between us when our paths crossed at restaurants and coffee chops. Although the grief had subsided, there was still a corner of my heart that longed for reconciliation, but I had resigned myself to not dare hope for what seemed like an impossible possibility.

It wasn't until COVID arrived that the Lord brought us surprisingly together at a coffee shop one afternoon. God opened a window for us to talk honestly and listen charitably. We shared our losses, which were many. Somehow, all the problems from our past seemed to pale in comparison to where we were now. All the ministry philosophies we had once so vigorously defended felt like long forgotten squabbles between young boys on a school playground. When we parted, tears had been shed, prayers had been prayed, and forgiveness had been granted. As you can see, the process was not fast. Because sometimes, repentance comes slowly. And with that repentance comes a slow love that God has been kneading in us without us even knowing it.

He is not slow. But He is slowing us down to become more like His Son.

Hope in Him.

PAUSE, PONDER, AND PRAY

WE DO NOT HAVE

For we do not have a high priest who is unable to
sympathize with our weaknesses, but one who in every
respect has been tempted as we are, yet without sin.
HEBREWS 4:15

Most of us have likely had the experience of a person who, for whatever reason, was not able to sympathize very well with us. Maybe it was a friend who couldn't seem to understand the trial we were going through, and we feel personally hurt and misunderstood by their lack of ability to empathize. But then there are those faithful friends, those rare and loyal companions, who willingly step inside all of our messes and sit compassionately with us through our confusion and crisis. Even when they haven't personally experienced what we're going through, they lend a listening ear, offer an outstretched arm, and provide a much needed presence in our pain.

As amazing as some of our close friends are when it comes to sympathizing with our weaknesses and temptations, they will never hold a candle to how deeply and perfectly Jesus is able to sympathize with us. Pause on that for a moment, if you would. We have a high priest, an intercessor who sits at the right hand of our heavenly Father. What we *do not have* is One who has separated Himself from the anguish of our humanness. What separated Jesus from the Israelite high priests is that He walked in the same shoes as the people He ministered to but as the sinless Son of God.

Imagine what this means for you and me who are confronted with an endless cycle of hard-to-resist temptations that are as relentless as they are irresistible. Imagine what this means as you consider your beloved friend and high priest. It means that Jesus, the spotless lamb who came to atone for the sins of the world, "gets you." One of the things we look for in a friend is someone who "gets us." They know us for who we are so there's no need for any posturing. We can be vulnerable because we have a friend in our corner who suspends judgment and just listens. We don't have to feel shame because we have someone who sees us and accepts us even at our absolute lowest.

Of course, there are limitations to this because none of our friends can sympathize with us without sin. So imagine, for a moment, someone like Jesus knowing exactly what you went through because He went through it too but didn't cave into the temptation like you and I do. Because He never gave into the temptation, He has a particular, one-of-a-kind heart for you that is untainted by the sin your human friends are susceptible to. It means His love for you is unprocessed. It means His compassion for you is full. It means His joy for you is boundless. It means His forgiveness for you is all-encompassing. As much as others can sympathize with your weaknesses, they can't offer you what Jesus our high priest can offer. This is the kind of high priestly friendship you need.

As Christmas is now only days away, and the new year beckons, maybe you find yourself at a deficit when it comes to people who are able to sympathize with you. You feel unheard and unknown as January 1 inches closer by the hour, mocking you with its icy, impending, and imminent approach. The truth might be that nobody has any conception of the year you have had. Nobody has any knowledge of the trepidation that consumes you as all of Christmastime sparkles surround you. Nobody considers that this season of joy has been a season of considerable sorrow for you that has been concealed behind all of this cheerful merrymaking.

Now consider this: the sympathetic and empathetic heart of Jesus. In every respect He has gone through what you have gone through. In all the ways you have failed when it comes to temptation, He has been faithful. His faithfulness is the very thing that covers your shame-filled failures, paper-thin faith, and Mount Everest-like fears.

> In all of your inabilities and instabilities, He is able and willing to stand close.

> In all of your insecurities and vulnerabilities, He is able and willing to stay close.

Like a shepherd who will carry you forever.

So rejoice, for we do not have a God who will do anything other than this.

PAUSE, PONDER, AND PRAY

AND NIGHT WILL BE NO MORE

And night will be no more. They will need no light
of lamp or sun, for the Lord God will be their light,
and they will reign forever and ever.
REVELATION 22:5

I gotta tell you, I'm so grateful to have so many things in common with my wife. We love to read great books, hike scenic trails, eat good food, laugh like crazy, and go slightly overboard decorating the house for Christmas every year. One of the things we don't share in common is my love of a brightly lit house.

What I mean by that is the first thing I do after I wake up in the morning or when we get home at night is turn on as many lamps and light switches as possible. I'm the opposite of the stereotypical dad who goes from room to room angrily turning off all the lights in the house. I *love* a brightly lit house! It cheers my soul. Of course, my wife Melissa would tell you the same, but she doesn't feel the need to have every light in the kitchen, living room, and library on all at once to achieve it.

When I think of the new heavens and new earth that the book of Revelation gives us a brief glimpse of, I think of it as the brightest and most beautifully lit place our eyes have ever seen. I think I have good reason to believe that too, especially when you consider that it will be the light of God that replaces our former need for lamps, light switches, and the sun. I think we can safely assume that this will be no dimly lit world!

If you're still unsure, think back on the light of Moses's face after he had spent time conversing with God on Mount Sinai and how he had to wear a veil because his face was too bright to behold.

For the Lord God will be their light.

And not just light to see the next foot in front of us so we don't stumble but the light of illumination. We will "know fully, even as [we] have been fully known" (1 Cor. 13:12). All that has been hidden will be revealed by the light of the Lord God. All the internal darkness our hearts have been immersed in will be lifted and replaced with the beautiful, shame- and guilt-lifting light of God. Imagine the astonishing clarity and warmth of such a light.

And night will be no more.

Like I said earlier, I don't enjoy a dimly lit house. It's not that I can't see anything; it's that it puts a shade on the room that feels like the equivalent of a dark and overcast sky. It becomes a place I'm not drawn to or want to spend much time in. But the light and illumination of Christ that we will one day live under can be experienced even now, as God gives us glimpses of it through the reassurance of the Holy Spirit in our hearts. The God who loves us is a God whose light is never obscured by the darkest night. Whatever your eyes are unable to see, God sees with undimmed clarity.

> If I say, "Surely the darkness shall cover me, and the light about me be night," even the darkness is not dark to you; the night is bright as the day, for darkness is as light with you. (Ps. 139:11–12)

Has the radiant sparkle of Christmas only illuminated the reality that you are stepping into a New Year that contains far more darkness and obscurity than you care to admit? Does January feel like entering a world without the sun, where there is no clarity of direction and no vision for what lies ahead? Well, from your vantage point, everything you're feeling may be true. Because the truth is, we don't know the sickness and sadness or the pain and perplexities that may be lurking around the corner come the New Year. What we do know is that not knowing a thing leads to greater faith in the something we do know, which, in our case, is the Someone we know.

I remember when I was a child learning how to swim, and my grandpa would have me jump into the shallow end of the pool to get used to the water. Every time he would catch me, and I would be safe. All I could see was that frightening water, but I didn't consider the fact that all he saw was my face because the water was no threat to him. It was impossible for him not to catch me with my four-year-old feather-weight frame. It is impossible for God not to see all the things you can't see and aren't meant to see for the sake of your ever-strengthening, ever-enduring faith.

Let me say it like this: the darkness can't make you invisible to God. It can't make you obscure to the one who *dwells in unapproachable light*, as the apostle Paul told Timothy. His presence is as piercing as the lightning that cuts like a neon knife through the night sky in an electrical storm. To God, the darkness is just as illuminating as the light is to us.

Bask in this light.

PAUSE, PONDER, AND PRAY

PEACE AMONG THOSE

Glory to God in the highest, and on earth peace
among those with whom he is pleased!
LUKE 2:14

What a beautifully vivid and artistic passage from the angelic voices of Luke 2, huh? The image of a choir of angels announcing the birth of the Savior can feel like the stuff of myths and legends, and yet to believe in a supernatural birth requires us to believe in a supernatural announcement of that birth.

What's the first thing that comes to mind when you consider that night so many years ago? Perhaps you think of those poor, unsuspecting shepherds watching this scene unfold miraculously before their eyes, not knowing what on earth to think. Personally, I've always been struck by the line "with whom he is pleased!" I might be showing my theological convictions here, but I love how the angels describe peace—that it is for those with whom God is pleased. What pleases God? Well, it's not sacrifice, we know that. King Saul made some unauthorized sacrifices to God one time that the prophet Samuel told him was, and I paraphrase, not cool. God makes clear throughout Scripture that He doesn't want our sacrifices but the sacrifice of our obedient hearts. An obedient heart is the only heart God can be pleased with and therefore have peace with.

How do we gain obedient hearts that please God? That's where the glorious gospel comes in. The birth of Jesus, the life of Jesus, the death of Jesus, and the resurrection of Jesus made it possible for God to have *peace among those with whom He is pleased*. However hard this is to hear, the truth is that we are born with hearts that have no peace with God because they are unredeemed and unwilling to surrender to Him. It is not until God in His grace brings us to the end of ourselves and we repent of our sins and trust in the work of Christ on the cross that we enter into a peaceful relationship with God where He is pleased with us.

On this Christmas Eve, pause and reflect on the grace God showed mankind by sending His Son to be an obedient sacrifice for you. Think of the possibilities it has opened up for you: peace with God, a loving relationship with Jesus, and a sure hope in this life and the life to come. It's helpful to remember that these shepherds didn't return to a life of ease after their angelic visitation. There would still be long, shivery nights tending their flocks by the light of the moon. They would still be people who were not highly thought of due to the nature of their lowly vocation. Yet there would always be this one glorious night when the unimaginable happened and everything changed forever. They may have returned to the same vocation, but they didn't return as the same shepherds. They returned glorifying and praising God for all they'd seen and heard.

What will you return to after the glory of the holiday season has passed, when it becomes a fading memory in your aging consciousness once again? Will you return like these unremarkable shepherds, glorifying and praising God for the remarkable love He has poured into your hearts through His Spirit? Will you remember that because of Christ's supernatural visitation to Bethlehem so many years ago, all the sorrow and suffering that have visited you in your life will, like an unwanted intruder, never be given entrance again. This is the kind of infinite, everlasting peace God is pleased to give the person with whom He is pleased.

See, these shepherds were not the men they once were before the angels appeared to them on a night that would live on in the stories and traditions that would be shared forever. They were not the men they once were before they unknowingly inspired the innumerable hymns and choruses that contribute to the richness of Christmastide traditions. They were indistinct men who had a distinct peace with God because they had a God who was pleased with their obedient hearts. They were men of humble estate who had been given hearts to match their trade as humble herdsmen. May our hearts be humbled anew by the peace-giving love of our humble Savior as we enter this New Year renewed by the God who is among us.

And ever so near.

PAUSE, PONDER, AND PRAY

GOD WITH US

*"Behold, the virgin shall conceive and bear a son, and they
shall call his name Immanuel" (which means, God with us).*
MATTHEW 1:23

Not a lot has changed for me over the years. I am the type of
person who absolutely loves having family, friends, and people
around me, especially during the holidays. I realize I might be in the
minority here, but I love a good old-fashioned Christmas party. The
kind that has oodles of appetizing food, delicious drinks, decadent
desserts, Johnny Mathis on the turntable, and colorful lights twin-
kling merrily around the tree and on the mantle. Sure, I may have the
"advantage" of being an extrovert to handle all of this frightening and
exhausting people'ing, but finding a quiet place in the corner has never
been my jam (although perfectly okay if it is for you).

I crave the comfort and camaraderie that come with rubbing
shoulders, engaging in conversation, and finding ridiculous things to
laugh heartily about. Whether it's my wife, daughter, a close friend, or
even just an acquaintance, having flesh-and-blood folks around gives
me a particular kind of joy as well as a reminder of the promise that
God will "never leave . . . nor forsake [me]" (Heb. 13:5). I'm hoping
this resonates with you, even if you are an introvert, and the lack of

alone time during the Christmas season can send a few shivers up your spine (ask my wife!).

Reflect with me for a moment on the above passage from Matthew. Think about the name of Jesus—Immanuel—and the kind of hope His name promises to us from this prophecy in the book of Isaiah. It is astoundingly warm and inviting, isn't it? Of all the things that could be said about Jesus, keeping in mind that the apostle John tells us that "the world itself could not contain the books that would be written" (John 21:25), the one thing in particular that Matthew mentions about the name of Jesus is that it's a name indicating His closeness to us. Given the endless adjectives that could have been used to describe Jesus, this is significant. This is not just "almighty God from heaven," "second person of the Trinity," or "Creator of the universe" Jesus, but "the God who is with us." Those other names we have to describe Jesus are good and true and need to become ingrained in our hearts so that we have the fullest picture possible of the person and work of Jesus. But every year, when Christmas comes around like clockwork, the name of Jesus we are reminded of most is *Immanuel*, which means "God with us."

God, in His steadfast love, new morning mercies, and grace upon grace, didn't *only* send us a powerful King to be Ruler over our lives. He didn't *only* send a Savior to atone for our sins. He didn't *only* send us a Son who made peace for us with God before packing His bags and returning to His heavenly abode to kick up his feet for all eternity. God sent us a person with a name who committed Himself to His followers to the degree that He said, "Behold, I am with you *always*, to the end of the age" (Matt. 28:20, emphasis added).

Today, as we've reached the pinnacle of this impossibly busy Christmas season, where you've barely had time to exhale, take a moment with me to breathe out slowly. Go ahead, do it again. Maybe even try it with your eyes closed. Remember that Jesus used the word "always" to describe just how long He plans to be with you. How might this be a balm to your exhausted soul as you think ahead to the innumerable challenges that lay before you in the New Year?

In all of your shaky finances, He is with you.

Through all of your fragile relationships, He is with you.

With all of your inability to repair the brokenness that surrounds you, He is with you.

It turns out that the old song is true after all, "The hopes and fears of all the years are met in thee tonight."

So whatever noise is raging around you—internally or externally—remember the One who is surrounding and covering you in all the chaos, for He is the bright light in all the bluster and the bright hope through all the havoc.

You don't only have a God; you have Immanuel, the God who is with you.

So Merry Christmas, if there ever was one. And there is.

PAUSE, PONDER, AND PRAY

Be sure to check out Ronnie's Christmas album

available wherever you listen to music